TURNED NOTHING INTO SOMETHING

The Indelible Pages of a Solitude Mind
Self-published
Editor SRJ
Copyright © 2025, by Hannah Kanavel

All rights reserved.
No part of this publication may be used, reproduced, or published in any matter whatsoever without the prior written permission of the publisher.

Title: The Indelible Pages of a Solitude Mind

International Standard Book Number
ISBN (Hardcover): 979-8-218-67873-9
ISBN (Softcover): 979-8-218-72686-7

Library of Congress Cataloging-in-Publication Data
LCCN (Hardcover): 2025914573
LCCN (Softcover): 2025909608

To those who are loved and to those who are lost..

As I write this, the book is entering the stages of completeness. It has been pushed back and rewritten many times. For it is my first born I feel never ready to release into the eyes of the world. The fears of my words not being understood to their fullness. As time has shifted forward I have realized that this is what true art is. Art is to be seen and interpreted. A collection filled with self discovery, self hatred, heartbreak, confusion, love and every emotion that comes with a solitude mind.
This collection of indelible moments
forever in their place.
I welcome you the reader the freedom to relish over
The Indelible Pages of a Solitude Mind
for it is no longer mine..

Contents

i wish you were still alive, that you didn't have to die

I Fucking Hate Funerals

War is a Crime

foreign

Easy

Walls of 1239

Planted Absolution

Color Me In

I Have To Remind Myself

No Trespassing

All I Do

Sits Between My Ears

Stuck In The Clouds Never Coming Down

sorrow

Sleep Tight

Different Perspectives

Sally

~~You~~ Her

Means Nothing

Last June

Three Then Nine

Remains Unsent

Track Three Sounds Like Me

In My Dreams

Like Patti Smiths'

before the fall

Love to David Jones

nonsense, make it make sense

To Me

Nothing To Say

Won't Lose Love

For You

Maybe They Were Right

Doldrums

This

the cows will never come home

Wasting My Youth

Haunted Solitude

Moments

One of My Biggest Regrets

still

Politician Problems

Telling Myself

newest craze

RECIPROCATED

You Will Never Know

Another Book Review

Tell me a sweet lie

Acidity

Last Night

Eight Pages Left..

September

down by the shore

Never The Same

Sometimes I Think

Silver Rose

to be me

One October Night After Midnight

love of my life

I wait in solitude

James Wright

Attach The Fragile Label
Another Shit Poet
Grocery List
Plot Twist
mournings in manhattan
already in my grave
Tough Luck
Philistine

THE
INDELIBLE
PAGES
OF A
SOLITUDE
MIND
A COLLECTION OF POETRY

i wish you were still alive,
that you didn't have to die
the days turn into nights,
that turn into years.
i feel ashamed,
when the days feel longer than years.
i fell stagnate.
eighteen forever, it's unfair you know.
i wish you were still alive,
that you didn't have to die.
while i think of suicide.
i wish you were still alive,
that you didn't have to die.

I Fucking Hate Funerals

In a home filled with no empty seats we stood back in the hallway by the walkway. Looking in with her in my vision I keep my head down. She kept crying holding on to whoever would hold her back. I stood there nauseous as hell. This kind of thing has always been strange. I guess I'll never understand it. There were many tears for many different reasons: loss, despair, disbelief, anger, and sadness. Those emotions broken up in between fond memories that would make us all laugh. Then the harshness of reality would sink in and it would have us crying again. Tony said to me that I should do what I am "good" at. I think he knew that I would be lost, that I was lost. That everyone would be lost.. without her. It was our turn. After her sister had spoken a few words. I could tell she was nervous trying to hold it together, she did it well. You have a great sister- great sisters.

With silent tears falling down and a shake of my chest. I patted your back and stepped outside passing everyone with cloudy vision. When I got outside I took a deep breath, calmed myself down. I stood at the front by the white pillars, waiting for them to come out. As I waited Haley came out with tears rushing down, her face colored red. I was never close with any of her other friends, but she came out alone, just like me. In that moment I knew she needed someone, I don't remember how long I hugged her or what I said when we pulled away, if we even said anything at all. I hope it helped her as much as it helped me.

It was a terrible fucking day.
Year.
Two years.
Three years
Four years,
and
counting..

War is a Crime

I guess they haven't heard about Floyd's blue sky.

It is pointless. Why haven't we learned this?

history repeating

history repeating

history repeating

Why haven't we learned this? It is pointless.

I guess they haven't heard about Floyd's blue sky.

foreign

my head aches

i have become a bore- a chore

there's a war going on inside

i have to decide

i might die,

that's fine

i am the highest i have ever been

but i am still small

cascading down

i didn't drown

i don't know how

walking back to buckle street

my heart aches

this is not what London

is supposed to be about

Easy

It feels so easy when it comes to you,
is this what it feels like to be in love- to feel free.

Walls of 1239

My words are written on the walls
He asked, "If this is what I really feel?"
I shook my head no.

My words are written on these walls.
"Is this how I really feel?"

My words were written on those walls,
now in this book.

And
that's
how
I
really
felt.

Planted Absolution

flowers enchanted by a vase
on a table made of glass
comes an intrusion
of a box containing fags
it is placed quickly with knowing blue eyes
coffin nails dancing inside

the box stays for awhile
gripped by faux stems
they speak hushed whispers
of keep it downs
so they are not found
the screams are not quiet
for they are caught inside the
valves of a pure heart

the house shivered plucked from within
by long skinny limbs
taken by hand held by mouth
a face uncertain masking a frown

wonders of bewilderment are present
not understanding one another
but their movements louder than
speaking sounds heard,
only one side will fold.

burned roots
severed again are a noose
intrusion after intrusion
the flowers welcome their intruder home
a maroon tub brimming with absolution

silver spoons
unearthing
uprooted
in breath petals twisted
the lung poison has drifted

replanted roots begin to overgrow creating
a catacomb protection from down below
intrusion after intrusion
the earth welcomes their intruder home

Color Me In

Keep me close them closer.
Pretending to be innocent but
so full of shit.

Not a saint, but I think before I speak.
Couldn't be the enemy,
she has befriended me.

Playing for keeps, still keeping peace.
No pool, no boat.
Can't keep you afloat.
What does she keep me around for?
Picked me so you wouldn't drown.
A one way ticket can't come back down.
Felt pawned.

Went so far, send me a postcard.
I'm not the enemy,
while you're next to me.
You walked the line
won't apologize, antagonize.

Keep telling me how you miss me,
it's clear in the way you treat me.
When I cried you didn't bat an eye.
Asked if I was okay when
you knew I was dying.

Can't stand to see me sad
but color me in shades of blue.
You still care, but it's twisted
in the way you do.

Echoes of their silence,
patiently waiting they make sound.
The reaction you wanted, you didn't get.
You threw it in my face, so
I'd never forget.
Distance made me realize,
I'm fine this time, no compromise.
The words they speak next
don't matter.
Too late.

They said what they said
they "miss" me.
I said what I said "I bet."
They said, what they said together.

Only myself to blame.
It made me over think,
and repeat.

I didn't tell them to say
what they said
But I let what they said
tell me how to live.
I
let
them
color me in.

I Have To Remind Myself
Freddie told the truth when
he said too much love will
kill you too bad I listened
too late but the world is
filled with so much
hate they try to get
us to medicate so
we can meditate
everyone can
relate it
seems
like
fate
but its
not to
late

No Trespassing

Falling in love with

what could have been

is dangerous territory.

It seems fun

ignoring the warning signs,

till you are the wonderer on the other side.

All I Do

If all I do is *love* you...

then that's pretty great.

Sits Between My Ears

I'm too much in my head,
I lie too much in this bed.
Thinking about what hasn't been said,
it's all in my head.
I'm running out of time.
This heart is cold, it's midnight.
Waiting for everything to be alright.

I can't get out of my head.
I can't get out of my bed.
My brain is tired,
it has been wired.
I can't count on anyone around.
I'm stuck in my head, losing friends.
Why can't I be fine?

This underlying disease,
I can't feel my knees,
I beg them please.
I feel the sun creeping in.
Don't sleep now my friend,
it's awakening again.

I can't get out of this head,
I can't get out of this bed.

We don't get any peace,
even when we sleep,
we
still
dream.

Stuck In The Clouds Never Coming Down

Oh,
what I would do for us
to laugh again.
I would float around a bit with you,
laying on a cloud for a laugh with you.

Fighting demons, slaying dragons
for a laugh with you.
A ticket to the end of the rainbow,
so I can slide down to where we were
for a laugh with you.

Before all those moments turned into yesterdays,
I'd float around a bit with you.

I'd cook for you
a table for two
just like I used to.
A glass of wine has taken its place.
For I have aged, while stuck in time.

I'd float around a bit with you,
laying on a cloud for a laugh with you.
A moment in time,
forever captured in my mind.
That's where it remains,
where it can be kept safe.
Never coming down from you.

sorrow

is the only word to describe how i feel
the dream i had been dreaming became a reality
though it was quickly diminished-
only by my mind, my body
music got less loud
cars drove slower
words were spoken softer
the world slowed down
but only for me
i mourn for my loss
and not only for this loss
but for all the other losses
as the world continues to turn
and i continue to move
i mourn for my loss

Sleep Tight

i know your heart is aching,

from what's been taken

carrying twice the weight it should be

you carried me

letting it go through song and raspberries

halen striped shorts are hard to miss

bare feet on the kick

my hearts hurting

my eyes are burning, i feel sick

sleep tight tonight

Taylor,

I know your lights not faded.

Different Perspectives

I was small, everything was big
looking through a magnifying glass,
running through grass
planting flowers with spoons
white bread, over easy eggs
memories have a white haze
like a dream, I never really lived at all

I am big, everything is small
looking through a kaleidoscope
all the colors collide
living nomadically through time
writing something that rhymes
blurry vision, no plans on sunday's
yesterday and today feel like a maze
like my dreams, I never really lived at all

I feel so small.

Sally

Room one-o-two not far from the lake o-so-blue.
Sits by the window, prefers coffee over tea.
Sally asks, "If I have a few minutes to speak?"
She doesn't know which way is home,
I remind her.

Looking from side to side
reading the numbers on the wall.
Looking back confused, less then a minute
she has forgotten where she is headed.
I know her routine and my own.

Here by three, coffee over tea.
They say, "She has gotten better."
but her mind has left her.

~~You~~ *Her*

You told me you would come,
but you did not show.
Hurt me more than you know,
it was the last time.
You did not know.

You told me you would come,
but you did not show.
I did not need you to come for me.
It was not about me.
It was not about you.

It was about her,
it will always be
her.

Means Nothing

Your
silence
has spoken
louder than words.

Your
silence
confirms my
doubts within you.

Your
silence
changed me,
because of your silence,
I hated me.

Last June

Everything was fine while
the birds sang a beautiful
tune of wedding bells
in the afternoon.
Last June

A sky painted blue,
heavy with sunlight.
The air was hot, dry.
Filled with dancing laughter.
Last June

The sky turned cold, gray.
Heavy with clouds full of rain.
All the flowers bloomed,
and left with you.
Last June
it tore me in two
last June
it went with you

Three Then Nine

I'm in hell
Where time is standing still, moving fast.
I'm in hell
Where the air is sweet, the grass is green.
I'm in hell
Where the flowers bloom pink, on the brink.
I'm in hell
Behind my shadow, a stagnant tease.
I'm in hell
Where the air is thinner, so I'm I.
I'm in hell
Same day over, and over.
I'm in hell
In the same place, maybe they were right.

I have put you in this box.

I have put myself there, everyone is in a box.

I wish I never was.

I wish I never did.

I hope I never will.

I have been dying to tell you.

Though we haven't talked in a while,

I understand.

I hope you do too.

Letter Remains Unsent

Track Three Sounds Like Me

He sits right beside me
a telescopic man
crawling into my head
on a voyage to my brain.
Sitting behind my eyes he hears
what sits between my ears
he wrote;

In

a

far

and

distant

galaxy..

Meet

   me

      where

         I

           dream

              where anything can happen

and

   then just then

      we

         will

           meet

              again in a dream

In My Dreams

Like Patti Smiths' four part poem says;

"fuck you"

before the fall

it makes no sense at all.
looking at the ceiling, eyes dancing with tears
you are in trouble
the end is near
though they do not mind
before the fall they "never knew" at all
they will think you are safe and sound because
they drowned you out
acting surprised like they never heard you scream
but they knew before
before it all
before the rose colored bath
worried about the mess they will have to clean
or about what god thinks
before you took your last breath
before it all
they knew
but the shame is still on you
even after the fall.

Love to David Jones

forever in peace

up in space or where ever you feel safe

i hope you see english evergreens,

no more dying trees

i hope you have air

to breathe

to sing

to dance

to feel free

forever in peace

nonsense, make it make sense

Too many people who are or aren't afraid,
we are the same.
Too many people here today
not enough the next.
What is wrong with the human race?

Scared to go outside.
Feels like it might be the last time.
Scared to go outside.
How can we live our lives?

Killed a man, who killed a man.
You think that's okay,
praising him till this day.
Isn't that strange to put a bullet in their brain?

Children fighting wars that aren't their own.
Begging to be fed instead high on
gunpowder- cocaine
How did it become this way?

They drugged a man who drugs many
just to get paid.
Isn't that insane to look the other way?

Seventy years later,
proof of innocence became clear.
After you watched George die in the electric chair.
What is justice when the damage is done.

In her house, in her bed.
In the streets, the color of skin.
What's going on in your head?
Playing pretend.

It's quite clear, it's worn on their uniform.
Taking an oath.
It don't mean that much, you pick and choose,
when it's convenient for you.
Another countless coward confesses
'This is not America'.

Brown skin makes them terrorists.
So kidnap them put em on a plane
take them to another country,
now it's out of your hands.
Whatever makes you sleep at night.
No matter how well you scrub
your hands aren't clean
Mr. President you are a bitch
with a sales pitch.

It's a thrill, going in for the kill.
Walking out, standing by your side.
He said, "He's hungry."
You offer him a ride with a free side
of burger king fries.
He said, "he had no choice, that
nothing was being done."
Look at what you've done.

The sound ringing through our ears
piercing our bones
we bleed

hearing each other scream
it's another tragedy
crawling through the tv screen
the color red it's just past ten
they will never go home again.
Another bad dream illusion running
from pensive silence.

Avoiding white t-shirt moments,
woke up could not breathe.
My heart is racing,
Theres a war going on outside,
not metaphorically in my mind this time.
White t-shirts turned red

Blamed Brian when it wasn't him.
Fell back to religion,
when they were killing them.
The homosapien influence
is always to blame.

Make it make sense,
all this fucking nonsense.

To Me

You are so beautiful to me,

I will try to stay beautiful for you.

Please stay this way.

Please don't go away.

Please don't change.

I always want to feel this way.

Nothing To Say

I have been here before.. I have always thrown it away, until now. I am gonna keep this one. It is funny, as I have come to my last few moments of life
I have nothing to say.

Won't Lose Love

I lie in bed with her every night.

As I held her tight,

I told her everything would be alright.

Telling her not to give up on love.

It will come back; tenfold.

She knows this.

They won't win,

burdened with

too much hate.

She's

alright

this

way.

For you

I love you, I do.
I'd surrender everything,
for you.

For you to be complete,
and
full of love endlessly.

Maybe They Were Right

They told him who he was, who he was not.
Who he was, how he ended up this way.
Denied assumptions.
Denied everything..
While denying he never understood trying,
so he pushed it away, became afraid.
He never had his moments,
so he became ashamed.
Maybe they were right.
He did not know who he was
and never listened to himself.

They told her who she was, who she was not.
Who she was, how she ended up this way.
Denied assumptions.
Denied everything..
While denying she never understood trying,
so she pushed it away, became afraid.
She never had her moments,
so she became ashamed.
Maybe they were right.
She did not know who she was
and never listened to herself.

They told me who I was, who I was not.
Who I was, how I ended up this way.
Denied assumptions.
Denied everything..
While denying I never understood trying,
so I pushed it away, became afraid.
I never had my moments,
so I became ashamed.
Maybe they were right.
I did not know who I was
and never listened to myself.

Time passes and colors fade,
you and I are not the same.

Doldrums

I can feel it-

as the air turns cold like

the souls that surround me

I can feel it when leaves crunch as the

children play

I can feel it as dogs howl at the sky turning gray

I can feel it now as I sit here writing this

I think ignorance,

it could be bliss

I can feel it now as my

stomach aches

I can feel it now

my disgrace in this place

I can feel the whispers in the wind calling to me

I can feel myself pretend

I can feel it-

calling my name again

I would rather die than love like this.
I would rather die than live like this.
I think hell might be better than this.

This

the cows will never come home

i wanna runaway

i wanna hide

wanna get away from my mind

wanna getaway from whats inside

wanna runaway from myself

want to run like hell

want to silence my mind just for a short time

just a short time

i wanna runaway from myself

want to run like hell

tired of the pressure

never getting better

doesn't make me feel alive

i wanna die for real this time

Wasting My Youth

put your heart back on your sleeve,
put away your teeth
there's no point in being mean
cynical or clinical
it's criminal, you see?

call me a quitter
i thought it was safe
i havent been honest
don't get too close,
a non romantic overdose,
you'll lose
i have myself fooled

they tell you who you are
who you wanna kiss
how did it ended up like this
unable to be be close
feeling foreclosed

it might seem manic- pathetic
maybe even a little poetic
i always see it whats underneath
all the missing puzzles pieced

tired of them telling me how to live,
if i'll sink or swim
hung up fabricated
feeling outdated
not into
just out of tune
gum on my shoe
wasting my youth

Haunted Solitude

When the light caves in,
out come the ghosts.

Our shadows leave us,
we are truly alone.

Moments

I felt like these moments were forever.

They were just moments that came and went.

Now I am who I am after these moments.

And forever is not long at all.

One of My Biggest Regrets

You told me something that you knew to be true. I asked, if you were sure. You were confiding in me. I had the nerve to ask if you were sure, of course you were. I wish I wouldn't have said that. Now I am sure. Now I would have said okay, It's all okay isn't everyone a little gay..

Sometimes I wish I did not love him.
Then I think about how much I love him,
how much I love loving him.
And I love him *still.*

Politician Problems

No absolution in your
big white house,
safe behind the gate.
It's where they lie, in their self crowned heads.
Locked away like a king,
safe from the outside.
Scared for their lives.

Not alone in the devil's left hand.
Day dreaming, playing pretend.
Won't place your hand on the Bible,
Pretending to be a savior but you should
save us from yourself

Acting bigger than Jesus.
Spewing hate towards the human race.
Your qualities are not quite
presidential, it's evidential.
An 'American Dream' based upon a false reality
makes broken dreams a fucked up catastrophe.

Rich men laugh they'll say,
"If you play your cards right.."
Those cards have been dealt,
realize who's hand you have-
who the dealer is.

A poor man
can't play a rich mans game.
Those who realized their fate,
still reek of defeat.

Telling Myself..

You said I have "nothing to worry about" the words I am tired of hearing all of the damn time. Maybe you are right maybe they are right and maybe I think too much, but I never want to kick my own ass for knowing I was right all along.
Pulling petals off a flower, now I feel sick.
I don't want to tell myself I told you so,
but I don't want to tell myself no.

lungs of the world are in a blaze
selling out for the ***newest craze***
the happening happens
when you smoke out all of
what you need to breathe
take their only home,
and wonder why they roam
trying to find a new place
to call their own
it amazes me how
selfish we can be..

RECIPROCATED

Non reciprocated love is viewed as sad, it is viewed with empathy, it is viewed as "childish".
Most love when they know they will be loved back.
I think that the purest love is loving
without knowing or expecting it to be reciprocated,
but most are unwilling due to their ego.

You Will Never Know

I wonder what it would be
like if you died,
like you did a few times.

How different life would be.
I was not there but they told me
about the shade of gray.
How they came home crying.
How everything had changed.

No lines across your face,
how you just fell away.
Mouth to mouth,
hands to chest.

Trying to find what I saw the first time
Flicking through the pages
I go back to reread the lines
The pages I created can not be found
Falling for what could have been
Though you are not at fault for that
Searching for you in a dictionary had me
thinking I was not intelligent
I feel elated to know something that you don't,
this is ***Another Book Review*** but of you.

Tell Me a Sweet Lie

You tell me a lie to make me stay.
I don't have to ask, because all
you do is talk anyway.

You tell me the sweetest of lies.
You will whisper my demise,
until the day you die.

You never whisper my way,
because you're not that brave.
It's okay its all lies anyway.
You blame me.

Angel in disguise whispering
my demise
trying to hypnotize
she speaks to me..

Acidity

the words on my tongue are not poetic

more like acidic, so I shall save my breath-

as i watch you eat your words it makes me a bitch

Last Night

As I reminisce back to that time
everything is now crystal.
Those two kids were not meant to be together.
Stumbling drunk no one knew what was coming.
I watched you discard all the
toppings on your pizza.
Stumbling drunk I kissed you.
I love you, I still do.
I'll forever need that moment.
It will last only in my mind.
Now that everything is over.
I will reminisce, it all makes sense,
your name forever on my lips.
As we spent our last night together,
we did not know it would be our last.
Our last
last night,
reminisced.

Eight Pages Left..

I wrote to you in a journal for years. I told myself that once those pages were filled, I'd stop. I'd move on. So I did stop. I stopped before I could fill the rest of the pages in hopes to prolong the feeling of letting go. I wanted to hold on for as long as I could. I still do. That's why this is being written in a different book so my pen doesn't taint the last few pages I have left. A way of holding on just a little longer. I am not ready. I am not ready to let you go, I am not ready to say goodbye to this part of myself. I am not ready to let all this go to feel completely alone.

September

failed deadlines
failed deadlines
september came and went
felt lost and hopeless
shattered and bruised
rain fell
went back to my roots
soon i began to bloom
september came and went
failed deadlines
september came and went
september came and went

You found yourself being weighed down about to drown, with rocks in your pockets wearing a frown.

Looking up at the sky, it makes no sense at all.
With no hand to hold to guide you home, the wind whispers in your ear cold and alone.

Clothes and shoes lay wet by the door, a reminder of how close you once were before,
there by the shore.

At the brink of changing time, turns out it doesn't taste quite nice, being alone in this space, time passes fast but slow it's hard to explain.

You feel it.
Every grain of sand, through your fingers it slips.
Falls with the wind, it leaves disappearing
with no where to go.

And when you find yourself back by the shore, I selfishly hope you think of me, because I think of you when I get the taste on my tongue.
down by the shore

What happens when what keeps you from the shore is just out of reach?

Never The Same

it comes back in flashes-
the day your heart stopped
indelible moments turning into these pages
i'd never imagined

everyday i wondered when you would call
i would wait around by the phone
but you were gone
no longer home
in my head we were just being petty
in my head you were still here

walking to your grandparents house
that was years ago
we would laugh till we cried for hours
about everything
and nothing at all
till we could not breathe
wondering when you would wake
so i wouldn't be alone

too young to be alone
too young to be asleep
too young to be a ghost

Sometimes I Think
Where did the hippies go?
Spreading peace and love.
Please don't tell me it was just the drugs,
when we need you the most.

Hippie love don't feel so close,
sometimes I have no
hope and I feel so alone.

Jim says, "hope is a begger, that
it walks through fire while faith
leaps over it."
Maybe that's true.

Time will fade and so will I,
our only guarantee is to die.
So we'll pick up every shade of
blue and tie our shoes.

Silver Rose

A ring of that you wear,
a silver rose.
Captured in time,
so many times.
Jones sir name of David.
A name I have taken,
made my own-
Silver Rose Jones.

blood on my hands

blood on my feet

dont like the way it feels

to be me

wore your shoes

they were too big for me

took them off

my bare feet

running through the grass

scraped my knees

the sky was blue

till it wasn't

the smoke was thin

till it wasn't

they say I wont

but ill do it

out of spite-

i'm commited

round and round we go

waiting for the undertow

i don't like the way it feels

blood on my hands

blood on my feet

One October Night After Midnight

You'll be alright tonight in this light
You'll make it out alive
Shadows appear to tell you some black lies–
they are just absences of light
Making mistakes that's what it takes to live life
It's after midnight, it's not black and white
Wrote it in the pages–
had a handful of reasons
The lights made them disappear for the night
It's after midnight but it's alright in this light
You'll make it out alive

tell him i love him,
because i'm too shy
and i'd lie

love of my life

As I wait,

I wait impenitently.

With a tight heart,

an aching feat.

Moving fast through

the tunnel, with blurry vision.

As I wait,

I wait in solitude

Crossing my heart, hoping I die

trying again in another life

because I am not losing this time.

As I wait, I wait impenitently in solitude.

I'll always remember *James Wright*,
I'll hold him tight in my heart tonight..

Another Shit Poet
Why should I try?
It is foolish, I know.
What would make a difference, no one knows.
What if I am just another shit poet..
So shit, so American, so..?

So I take the piss out on myself
before you can form your own opinion
throwing up in the back of the cab
made a mess of myself
I am a let down
my thoughts still haunt me
I wish I had left them at sea
but they followed me
it is different now
What if I am just another shit poet..
So I take the piss out on myself-
that I know.

Grocery List

Chicken

Lemons

Flowers

Chocolate

Everything feels like a waste of time when you don't want to be alive, time passes by.

Fettuccine

Parmesan

Garlic

Heavy Cream

Plot Twist

I can't do the
"how are you's"
the "I miss you too's".
I am not there,
I won't play pretend.
No communication
The sounds you make
don't matter you're too late.
It's too late.
I knew the gun was loaded.
I should have bit the bullet,
I should have knew it.
You were a twist in the plot
I never saw coming.
Broke my back and heart
dodging the bullet.
I should of knew it.

mournings in manhattan

not far above ground placed in 200 sq ft
between walls of white, the carpet blue
noise of the city invades my space
a man on the phone in room *613*
he speaks three languages into the early hours
of the next morning
could barely sleep
I guess what they say is true
this is the city that never sleeps

waking on sheets of white like the ones back
home except they are not my own
the sun shining from the east
no one come for me, please
no words have been spoken it is silent
I could get used to this
I could wake up like this forever, in room *612*

swimming through the waves of the radio
being outweighed by the noise of white
in their eyes with your disguise
it swallows me
feet are heavy never touching ground
drifting through the words that are spoken
making sound for reasons they don't know
lies unfold taking control
signaling smoke it calls out
i can't tell their voice from my own
in between my ears it gets tough
thinking it was enough
sinking down i will always be drowned out
suffering silence makes the stomach sick
out shined with praise of the simplest of things
walking on eggshells
attaching the label to your back-fragile
it will never be enough
sinking down
i will always be drowned out
in between my ears it gets tough

Tough Luck

rolled the dice with losing cards
my hands were tied, i had to fold
unchained, feeling framed
over selling my intelligence creating a mess
i am selfish, you don't have to tell me this
no one else beside me besides me
unvoiced opinions
mimed emotions provoke havoc
leads to unwell heads
dying to waive my white flag
to never speak a word to anyone again
succumbing to my injuries
disintegrating into the earth
this is my fate
already in my grave

I envy those who do not understand art.

The ones who do not need it.

Those who do not have anything to say.

The ones with no inner monologue.

Philistine

THAT WAS SOMETHING OR NOTHING

www.ingramcontent.com/pod-product-compliance
Lightning Source LLC
Chambersburg PA
CBHW040313170426
43195CB00020B/2961